ALSO BY ANGE MLINKO

Matinées

Starred Wire

Shoulder Season

Marvelous Things Overheard

DISTANT MANDATE

ANGE MLINKO

DISTANT MANDATE

FARRAR STRAUS GIROUX

NEW YORK

Farrar, Straus and Giroux

18 West 18th Street, New York 10011

Copyright © 2017 by Ange Mlinko
Printed in the United States of America

First edition, 2017

Library of Congress Cataloging-in-Publication Data

Names: Mlinko, Ange, author.

Title: Distant mandate : poems / Ange Mlinko.

Description: First edition. | New York : Farrar, Straus and Giroux, 2017.

Identifiers: LCCN 2016034933 | ISBN 9780374248215 (hardback) |

ISBN 9780374716141 (e-book)

Subjects: BISAC: POETRY / American / General. | POETRY / General.

Classification: LCC PS3563.L58 A6 2017 | DDC 811/.54—dc23

LC record available at https://lccn.loc.gov/2016034933

Designed by Quemadura

Our books may be purchased in bulk for promotional, educational,
or business use. Please contact your local bookseller or the Macmillan
Corporate and Premium Sales Department at 1-800-221-7945, extension
5442, or by e-mail at MacmillanSpecialMarkets@macmillan.com.

www.fsgbooks.com
www.twitter.com/fsgbooks
www.facebook.com/fsgbooks

1 3 5 7 9 10 8 6 4 2

TO MY LOVE (MY LUCULENT ONE!)

Damn it all! all this our South stinks peace.

. . . Let's to music!

EZRA POUND

Mordant au citron d'or de l'idéal amer.

STÉPHANE MALLARMÉ

CONTENTS

DISTANT MANDATE

COTTONMOUTH

A levitating anvil. Omen of seagull
Blown inland. Ranch gate said RIVERSTYX,
but it was the woodland that looked lethal:

no place to put down your foot. Bucolics
demand boustrophedon. The by-the-book.
"Male cicadas thrummed their stomachs

while a dragonfly eyed us from a pole hook.
Ripening grapefruit. Us just under.
Shoulder to shoulder. Tree-shook."

Milky skies belied the baffled thunder . . .
They left, not footsteps, *trails* in uncut grass.
"Like parallel snakes. No wonder."

Eurydice should have thought moccasins,
a.k.a. cottonmouths, apropos
stealth. Distilled to systole-diastole. Assassins.

And everywhere sharp palmettos
Clacked tongues in homage to language—
"I should have rhymed them with stilettos."

Why would E. shed her red wedge
with its Mary Jane band,
wetland mosquito and midge

circling ankle (punctuated, understand,
by the awl, to mimic ellipses . . .)? "Because"
—O.—"she mimicked the shy strand

of epiphyte—Spanish moss—
goose-pimpling the languid pond
with its dependent clause."

COOKED IN THEIR OWN INK

Byblos—unreclaimed by the sea
   through which it nurses
myth, grudges sand to its neighbors—
   is visited no more by goby,
gilthead bream, octopuses . . .
   Impresarios of fresh labors

have gone elsewhere, though
   orchards of pomegranate
and lemon flourish amid ruins,
   sepulchres repurposed, as though
a new dynasty to admit;
   like the melting down of coins,

bells, the material persists.
   First, Chinese scholars
abandoned far-flung pavilions.
   Alexandrian scribes; archivists
from Córdoba; illuminators
   of Celtic vellum; civilians

drafted into the holy orders
  of manuscript hoarders;
were next to come to Byblos,
  last resort and headquarters
for stylus-conscious courtiers
  and scriptural sibyls

at their philias, their alphabets.
  I know "it is here
that the banished gods are in hiding."
  Children chisel fridge magnets
of fish fossils off grottoes
  for tourists of writing.

[DEREK MAHON]

DENTRO DE LA TORMENTA

The revelry of others showed up as
bags under my eyes, flames in glassware
shooting up on this or that terrace
as my own transparent heresy.
The colors were either that of flora
or bath salts; neon was their oracle.
In our room above the café
the bass drops were abortifacient.
One child threw the curtain back,
squealing, "A Lamborghini Huracán!"
and the other, rolling a Matchbox car,
sharing in, then mocking, his ardor,
fabricated a sighting of a Porsche.
Dentro de la tormenta, I saw a woman
braced against wind like an admiral
shouldering ashore, sea foam bullish.
The swimmer was exuberant,
but I wouldn't particularly have wanted
to be that girl having to effect a rescue,
slight, thin-nosed, on lifeguard duty.

[MIAMI]

CAPTIVITY

If it's Yuletide in the New World,
then what bellies up to the manger
are rattler, gator, buzzard. Just as a
wooden snake in a basket of toys
at this barbershop I bring the boys
seems to hiss ". . . *es su casa*,"
I take the part of the friendly stranger
only where hair is imperiled.

Festive lights are strung up, arranged
around amusing headlines on the wall:
ROSENBERGS DIE (scissors flashing);
BIN LADEN KILLED (clippers gnashing).
And that's not all (no, that's not all . . .):
MAN IN TX JAIL CELL FOUND HANGED.

★

Horsemen of upcountry limestone,
Quahadis rode through sumac
that tore at the clothes and the flesh,

hunters to the bone.
Never touched a hair on the head
of their own or adopted child, fed
on half-digested sweet milk fresh
from a bison calf's slit stomach.

They didn't make laws, weren't a nation.
They had, all told, a common tongue.
They snuffed out Rachel Plummer's infant
(nursing was lost time); in that instant
she turned savage on her captors, won
unwittingly their admiration.

★

Corpses frightened Mary Rowlandson.
Yet "I must and could ly down," she'd write,
"by my dead Babe, side by side all the night,"
in the wigwam, weekuwom, wiquoam
which the child departed "like a lamb."
Though one bullet stitched both, yes,
she "left that Child in the Wilderness . . .
and myself in this Wilderness-condition."

Sold for gunpowder under the cones
and needles of New England tinder;

ate an unborn fawn: so "tender,
that one might eat the bones
as well as the flesh." Gentleness (I know)
is learned. And unlearned also.

★

Now the lines of his skull appear,
the hair fallen on the floor
(grown for the better part
—a thousand pardons—of a year
and as leonine as a roar;
a first attempt at body art,
a shine like a bubinga drum shell,
or the Earth Ride cymbal

now offered up as casually
as that head from Monkey Slough
mounted over the W.C.).
And as if it wasn't enough,
the aeolian origins of loess,
the ground a leonine mess.

★

It's Yuletide in the New World,
and the metallurgical fur of tinsel
warms the atmosphere;
the crèche with its inlaid pearl
canceling the blood on the lintel,
against long odds, will appear
as long as mothers house
golden apples in pine boughs.

And as if it wasn't enough,
the basket of toys yields a tortoise
that crawls away on its cutlery
much like the roughest of rough
drafts of our own migrant house,
Sheetrock bunker plus scullery.

★

And as if it wasn't enough,
hair fallen from the clipper's tines
might have been as rough
as the heaps left behind
of a herd, shorn. Or a horde,
advertising his assent
to the life of the horse and sword,
and to go wherever they went.

Buzz Cut 10, Bald Fade 16.
Fluffs the nape, dabs with the shaver,
underplays it as a "trim."
It's as if—the works of time undone—
the mirror, held up to him,
shows his moonface smaller, graver.

LEAN STEER

What's with the antique stores, the butterflies
and sunflowers rigged from scrap metal?
The sempiternal biergarten (alias
saloon) with the wide screens (football),

a spice-grinding abandon to the windup radio's
right-wing warm-ups? The hog-callin'
melismata of the local girl star's now going, *Adios*.
Where the tin flower's rust is read as pollen.

[ROSENBERG, TEXAS]

IN THE GODS

I was up in paradise, or "the gods,"
the cheap seats, a bird's-eye view.
The singers had joined hands
and surged toward the lip of the stage
while I, at the knee-high railing,
jumped to my feet, leading the ovation.
The line surged forward, I swayed;
it dropped back; we kept clapping.

My purse was bias or ballast.
I could pitch forward from the precipice
to the bottom of Nibelheim
or into the tanks of the Rhine,
drawing on my death-defying thirst
as high and low reversed.

Texas City smokes like a witch's sabbath.
And in the lanes feeding the ferry ramp,
autos accumulate, the heat feels like wrath
the dark won't damp. The goddess Erda
shudders the stanchions the freeways

are built on; a furrow appears
as she nears the surface toward Dallas,
bursting through in outcrops of clay.

The play, as it's called, varies in depth
from four to fourteen thousand feet.
Whatever dwarf dotes down there
on his light-catching ring, a trickster
fire god Loge casts an aboveground spell,
flaring waste gas on a new well.

There's more than one Valhalla
being built with the 27 percent royalty
on proceeds from the oil leases.
The force that forges gold differs from
the force that forges hydrocarbons,
differing from the force that forges love.
Gold is formed in the split second
of a supernova, oil over eons,
love in the window of an hour.
Erda knows what is past,
what is passing, and to come.
It lit me in the gods:
fracked with river water,
and piped into a rich contralto.

CYPRESS

I don't remember Galveston, the F-
150s prowling—Lone Star in hand—
the same sand as turtle and lizard,
kiddies with eyes in their buckets.
I don't recall the dolphins in thrall
to drilling rigs and intracoastal ships,
the odor of petroleum in the breeze,
down I-45 to the coastal refineries,
end-on-end car dealerships.
I don't remember that seawall,
sargassum weed heaved by trebucket,
who knows, thriven on fertilizer
in the runoff from the heartland.
Crosses all over, sans serif.

FRONTIER

A riderless ass gallops up to your wagon.
Your child is sleeping through the jolts.
It's a bad omen; it portends some kind of agon.

Camels, drafted into the Confederacy, are gone;
their Arab handlers intermarry with the slaves.
They could scare a Colt into your wagon,

trample fences, and into the bargain
cause mules to self-impale on barbed wire.
Tides rifle nautilus. The frontier agon

involves cholera and Karankawa jargon
in your kitchen, remanding sweet potatoes.
A Frenchman tries to hitch a camel to his wagon

but the beast of the qasida goes native again,
and breeds until hunting parties
guarantee reduction. Ergo: No more agon.

Even the horses hated its scent.
The Karankawa vanish into the Coahuiltecan;
But now a riderless ass gallops up to your wagon.
It's a bad omen. It portends a new agon.

They sang "Green, Green Grass of Home"
sailing west from New Orleans.
They sang "Ne me quitte pas" beneath mesquite

while digging graves in Matagorda.
Pelican soup was a vile, greasy potage.
They sang "Green, Green Grass of Home"

where alligator was a luxury (the meat)
down at the Turtle Bayou Turnaround.
They sang "Ne me quitte pas" beneath mesquite.

Near the Old and Lost River they surmised
Spanish moss strains coffee pretty good.
They sang "Green, Green Grass of Home."

They were whinging "Stuck in Lodi,"
forty Slavonians in the Big Thicket.
They sang "Ne me quitte pas" beneath mesquite.

They cut down the trees, they sawed the blocks,
split the blocks into billets, split the billets into boards.
They sang "Green, Green Grass of Home."
They sang "Ne me quitte pas" beneath mesquite.

Frederick Olmsted was right when he wrote
G.T.T. (Gone to Texas) was appended
"to every man's name who had disappeared

before the discovery of some rascality."
Brands were a language: Shanghai M, Running W.
Frederick Olmsted was right when he wrote,

or rode upright, through "a sort of Brobdignag grass."
Bradded L, Walking R, Swinging J.
Every man's name who had disappeared

singed like needles off a cactus, whiskers off rope
(this was a practice). Rocking T, Tumbling K.
Frederick Olmsted was right when he wrote

in the alphabet we got from the Canaanites.
Oxhead A, Camel G. If it doesn't brand, it bites.
To every man's name who had disappeared,

someone added: Sent to heaven to hunt for a harp.
Or maybe it was another case of slow.
Olmsted slowed so he could write while he rode
among men whose names had disappeared.

THE FORT

From the weathered boards knots pop
like the eyes of potatoes. From brick
salients not a clink of a pupil in a loop-
hole. Cannon, yes, but without their kick.

Ironically or entirely appropriately,
who can say, the fort will not admit us.
The reenactors are going home; we see
them retreat, backs x'd with sus-

penders, toward the forest housecleaned
into a state park. Ocean beyond the ramparts
suggests that stem-celled seconds fiend-
ishly agglomerate with fits and starts

into unprecedented forms. And so
who cares that the fort's built on a sandbar,
that we don't make it in, and go
only so far around the perimeter.

MILKWEED

It's August. Loosely we follow the arc
    of the monarch.
A pilgrimage north, a pivot, a *retorno*.
MONTREAL, where the earring on a bough
is genuine chrysalis. *Bon courage!*
The milkweed it's fed on renders it
poison. In lieu of camouflage.

Resources, by nature intestate
    abound underground the KEYSTONE STATE.
Above, the sanctuary of Asclepiadeae
(see milkweed) is twined with monarch larvae
(a stand-in for the healer's snakes) in its floss.
The forests are a trickery of acoustic baffles,
hemlock (not wedlock), fern and moss.

Though wedlock was not the toxic chalice
    given philosophers' wives, or Alice
when she shrank to a footstool's size,
reality must be what three, not two, apprise.
While a monarch heads toward VIRGINIA
(as do we), I indulge in that which is by
definition interesting to one: nostalgia.

Magnets in the antennae help orient
    the monarch, seemingly vagrant
but espoused to minuscule lodestones.
Mine gravitate to bittersweet zones
driven by memories, not instinct.
Driving through the heartland of sad songs
builds a contract stronger than the one we inked.

We're driving backward through the season—
    no more hint of gold on trees, on
wine-red stems along the roadway; in the South
it's still hot and florid as a tiger's mouth.
My dear, not one of these black-and-oranges
shows their offspring the whole route over gaps
in generations and mountain ranges.

LOUISIANA. The wind's cessation—let that stand
    for the cessation of the stained-
glass tatterdemalion in the grass
who alit on one of us like a sign of grace.
Loosely we follow the arc of the monarch
back to TEXAS, to our own backyard where I
planted milkweed—toward cessation of ache.

GELSENKIRCHEN

At some point they got off at Gelsenkirchen,
which is on the same train line as Hannover,
and while there, had their portraits taken.
That's all the sense I can make of this stopover
on their way to the coast, where the ships
were taking the faux Poles, the birchen people,
to whatever hospitable continent, on tips
circulating in the famine camps and steeple-
lands. Rotted frames, rusted nails, show their age:
the peeling backs, the glass glued now to them
like glass-topped coffins . . . the water damage
(my fault) that looks like ectoplasm.
Wherever they went they put icons side by side.
An embroidered linen cloth went over the top.
And so I place them, their calm looks borrowed
from those icons, and the photographer's shop,
"Im Lorenkamp," the historical clue I worry—
needlessly—since knowledge lives in imitation,
as in the train window, dark as boots and caraway,
they composed the mystery of salvation.

REVELATIONS

We could eat grapes half the morning like Goethe
hunkered against an obelisk,
waiting on the proper angle for the season
to see the Sistine sun-kissed,

or we could slip a coin in the device
that illumines another masterpiece
in a sordid chapel (soon again
dark shrinks it to a gleam of grease).

Time wedded Syriac to Hibernian.
I think of this when I raise my eyes
to a filigreed cross in a sanctuary
and in the roof beams recognize

the wooden hull of a small ship,
an upside-down caïque,
such as sliced the water near Cyprus
wedding Hebrew to Greek.

I raise my eyes to paintings retouched
with soot from countless tapers lit,
giving body, face, and fragrance
to the prayers of the desperate.

So that sfumato wasn't the artist's,
and the Latin wasn't Jesus's,
but the suffering belongs to all of us,
and the technique is the breeze's.

I think of the rustic Helens, Lydias,
Alexanders—for ages stranded
between the Urals and the Carpathians
—by Church Greek branded.

Dolphins escorted Goethe past chaplains.
He stopped short at the portals
to foam-haloed Patmos, to Thebes,
and their violet-haired mortals.

LISTENING POSTS

As these things go, it's fun
to watch my riveted son
fly an F-16 on a tiny screen
topographically green.

His speed on airstrips
achieves its own eclipse
as he sublimes into the blue.
Contrails spastically accrue

and the distance is so great
it traverses seemingly the state
of ecstasy, and nothing more,
to do with, say, the coming war.

★

Antennae of the listening post,
alight, seemed to scan for ghosts
amid the voices of the Med,
dust the mint and fennel fed.

Standing on the limestone rock
with family, run out of talk
as an hourglass its sand—
I waited to be gainsaid again

by any such ghost as would appear
to overturn my muted fear
and top off my head with hope
of tiny jewels speckling taupe.

★

Jets reduced to colored specks
and again from rex to wrecks,
project voices into space
of men in—not a suit, a case.

Meanwhile I, with sapphire
posts in both ears, beg to differ
if this sand-flourishing thistle
is not equally epistle

from the backyards of hackneyed
plant life we call weed.
It whispers of the coming battle
feeding dust to thyme and basil.

DAYS OF 1999

Aloe aloe   I mutely mock in French accent
the desert garden of Yves Saint Laurent

It's open to the public in Marrakech
Above, the date palms thresh

Below, carp weave the dirty water
in a pool the size and shape of carpets

(to fund their passage to Gibraltar
the Mauritanians on the parapets

sell magic ones) What a cobalt blue!
Made bluer hard by tangerine

But look   the shuttered villa comes into view
belatedly   because the bougainvillea overscreen

and this paint needs refreshing   *Sidi*
this out-of-fashion pied-à-terre's gone seedy

I'm from the loamy well-watered north
but imagine that this heat is creeping forth

from the greenhouse atmosphere
and soon these aloes will appear

in the places we're displaced from
and displaced again   so nomadic have we grown

we ought to have a yurt instead of home
We ought to have a camel with his water drum

How odd to be thought rich by all the touts
and yet this Saint Laurent buys a house

lets it rot while we live hand to mouth
in the precincts of the jet-set south

hearing over a half carafe we go halves on
"In Italy you can get fat on saffron . . ."

"THEY THAT DALLY NICELY

WITH WORDS MAY QUICKLY

MAKE THEM WANTON"

Should I take this time, while the children are in school,
to untrim the tree? Standing in the dish we let go dry,
it looks well preserved, as if Christmas were still
in our future; would it spare their feelings if I dismantle
piece by piece its grandeur, or will I amplify
their sense of loss, dejeweling it without ritual?

Epiphany, we drove by a painted camel on a church lawn
—or what, after a hard freeze, is lawn's avatar.
Jefferson Davis, no magus, brought camel brawn
to Texas to aid in the Civil War. Now they're gone
except in these tableaux where Balthazar,
with all his diamonds, kneels before the Paragon.

We were coming back from a weekend getaway
before the holiday's official end. I took the dog,
went out on the beach, but the length of South Padre

was swept by a long wind; dunes went astray;
thin snakes of sand grains slithered; I couldn't jog;
the Gulf went from glaucous to cauldron gray.

As in a Bedouin poem a gown of white sand
eternally receded before me; the snakes raced.
The profile of the island was changing, and
despite the fury in my heart that this tempest fanned,
the beloved's encampment can never be retraced:
all texts are unwritten by the same hand.

Boxes of baubles for yearly display we haul
faithfully from house to house no nomad, I realize,
could conscion. Your hem's circumference all
you know of enclosure. The open stall.
Patterns are starting to emerge to my wondering eyes—
on my skin, even. Up close, the epidermal

Alhambra of triangles, stars. Back of wrist. Kneecap.
Gypsies that named the lines on palms don't look
at soles, like yours, that close the lovelorn gap
between the territory and (yes, yes) the map.
Our tree is still in its vise. The road we took
(don't turn) is riddled with needles, dried sap.

The boys are lighting fireworks on the ground.
(Recall, this is a country called Illyria;
even stars are upside down.)
Toby and Andrew name the kinds of deliria:
jumping jack, blooming flower, black cat . . .

What rose-green shower—or umbrella—is that?
The empty lot Toby and Andrew bring us to,
where crablike diggers squat
inertly in the champagne-cold, is impromptu
beach, with all the night sky for sea. Juiced-

up Roman candles discharge into it. Loosed,
frantic spinners change color like salamanders:
spry Viola jumps back, goosed;
but Feste jokes about motley, and ganders
at the tracers that shroud us in gunsmoke.

(Perhaps it's just another carnival joke—
your hand on the small of my back? Like blooms
in the sky?) The New Year spoke
by spoke nears, but with a breath of tombs
the moment Feste, feeling insolently gay,

heckles a rather elderly personage: "Pray
you go out on your toes—or comatose."
I hear Malvolio say
to Olivia holding her sparkler too close,
"Back off—you're wearing too much hairspray."

Speaking of ground flowers:
Epiphany. The resorts are dead
but for the foreign powers
that raise pistils in a yellow head

crouching on a Cypriot beach.
A rough, hairy pod—surprise!
—jumps at my touch
and squirts seed at my eyes.

Because I hear the wind rush
against the palm-palms
with which our balcony is flush;
sky cloud over with qualms;

memories blur. Psyche's actuaries
beg to take the measure
of our folded white Januaries
with sleep's ruled erasure.

Do I have to be mailed in bubbles or
toiling over bouillabaisse,
frisées, port glaze for Sir Omnivore;

protagonist of a page-turner, Haze
mère or *fille*; people-pleaser, cocktease,
she-bear, in niqab, in getup, in stays;

having taken Saint Paul's advice to seize
the gold ring: Who groks to the paradox?
Though one would sooner burn than freeze . . .

I've taken to the dark stuff since you left:
a stovetop espresso maker with the heft

of a campfire kettle
to express more strongly my mettle.

Isn't love all this, all this mocks?

BREEZE BLOCKS IN THE

WILD HOLLYHOCKS

There should be a healthy trade
in sandbags. Cement should be
our chief export. Some of it's made
a stadium, some a prison. Slurry

is churned from the rainy season.
At any time, any number of yellow-
hatted helots surrounds one
volatile jackhammer or backhoe

askew on a quickening dune.
Shouldn't sand mute the machinery
steps away, as it had done
the massacre behind the scenery?

Blue sky like empty seats offsets
the soldier at the curve of the headland,
posed between—what else?—
sandbags, with his ammunition band,

AK-47, coded beret and bored
demeanor switching tack
to an Ides of March smile. Right side
of concertina wire, I smile back.

DECISION THEORY

"That reminds me: the low-key
Ottoman mansions from which
high-rises thieved the sea view
were bereft of any stitch
of arabesque: stained glass,
faience, even roof tile.
We often passed in a taxi a tree
bursting through a domicile.

If I sat anywhere long enough,
I became a vanitas,
giving the brush-off
to ants while gardenias
attracted business. Mysteriously,
I was getting friendly with S.
The wife of your colleague,
remember? The actress

who threw rambunctious parties.
And on the table, in the open,
left two or three boards

in medias res for her husband.
I hadn't heard of these fantasy games;
it explained why he would marry
a role-playing girl, and she him:
his métier was 'decision theory.'

After one of our first tête-à-têtes
I saw her on the street near her flat.
S.! I shouted, ran to embrace.
'Wrong person.' And the expat,
seeing me reel back a bit,
helpfully took her shades off.
But she looked more like S. than ever.
I drew back from my gaffe.

At a Christmas party chez S.,
I still couldn't shake the sense
that it had been she, and that I
was one of her experiments.
Ney, ney, ney, I kept thinking,
mesmerized by the Arabic flute.
S. was as friendly as before.
I felt like a dupe."

MARRIAGE AS BAROQUE MUSIC

"We ask that tonight you share a program."
Much of the crowd is older than I am.
Even older: this idea of love
consecrated in a cedar grove.
Komm, mein Heiland, mein Verlangen,
Komm von Libanon gegangen.
"Come, my Savior, my desire,
Come to me from Lebanon."

So Buxtehude's lyric goes.
Two singers. The soprano's
built like an ox; the mezzo-s's
highest note's topped by tresses
and there's an element of mirth
when, ignoring the other's girth,
she locks gazes with her, passionate:
Solomon and Sheba duet.

Furthermore, the theorbo—
strictly for the anachronism lover!
It keeps threatening to keel over,

an unanchored pendulum.
Pity the swain who's made
to pluck a serenade
while steadying, without a strap,
this metronomic member in his lap.

Because our hiatus is on hiatus;
because a friend, so hopeful for us,
left me two tickets at Will Call;
because music is physical—
we gingerly stay. Yet the program says
the sopranos and the violins part ways.
Uncertainty of what they'll sing
makes the composition interesting.

Here, as in Lebanon, gardenias bloom.
This time of year, they perfume
the taxicabs—and butchers' lintels,
mingling the sweetness of their smells.
They don't blush to return to the stark
fact of their pallor visible in the dark
—flattery you pressed on me, ages ago.
Remember? The marriage-scale.

It starts with *do*.

KNOT GARDEN

Like Benedick and Beatrice, I thought—
as we went around the garden
trying, with words, a precarious knot.

Trading barbs with my accomplice,
I pointed out the faded roses,
like Benedick and Beatrice.

I fingered one seeded clot
that would become a rose hip
hard as the primordial knot.

Below was the littered trick
of a once-glittering beetle
like Beatrice or Benedick.

The metal tags were polyglot
but the long arms of live oak
tied and untied a prelapsarian knot.

Millions or billions don't mean bliss;
think cotillions when you speak of stars
like Benedick and Beatrice

and not the prestidigitatory *not*.

HERSHEY SUITE

Arriving at the Hitchcockian hotel,
the Milton Inn,
one might have pictured Lucifer in Hell
what with the ice bin
busted in the swelter, unsigned landscapes
nothing could brighten:
not the tallowy pull-cord on the drapes
nor pool's reflection.

Namesake of Milton Hershey, not he of
Paradise Lost,
(much less *Regained*); no obstacle to love,
ourselves uncrossed.
But the Cockaigne of limitless chocolate,
bricked and sauced,
wrapped in gold leaf, a flag on its summit—
at that I paused,

thinking: *Their martyred blood and ashes sow*
O'er all th'Italian fields
(the other Milton, four centuries ago).

Antinomian PA yields,
as well as candy, cream and wool and grains;
and, crucially, shields
his descendants from religious campaigns
that ended worlds.

A replica factory in this pastoral
crushes fake beans
with brushed steel, utterly simulacral;
branded Halloweens
emerge from this maw, as if the plain fact
of horror streams
from a roller coaster, digestive tract
for swallowed screams.

Milton, meet Milton, though he hated rhyme
—and thus the sweet—
but maybe I exaggerate; his sublime,
you deviously submit,
was all in his wife, and would have wished
her here on this sheet,
its claim to cleanliness doubtful, yet swished
away by maculate feet.

BORROWED BIO

Where we'd recently lain,
exchanging a kiss,
stork consorted with crane,
   limpkin with ibis.

Was this as much wedding
as there would ever be,
the fowls' foot-webbing,
   the identificatory

ring around a throat?
Exchange of earth and air:
not a vow but a vote
   of confidence a feather

might tip by a single scale . . .
That one's a raconteur,
so much salt in his tale;
   this one's a countertenor,

lilting above the feast.
The archon of his hectare—
spotted—spotted least.
   Here's a little heckler . . .

Penciled seagull in the margin.
Following line by line
the path you took, I imagine
   no print so fine.

TWO HANGINGS FROM OVID

It is Hermes stepping off his winged sandal.
>   . . . *I saw the Writing Spider sitting with aplomb*

Even his caduceus, despite the scandal
>   *dead center her creation, above the compost*

of its forfeiture, lies abandoned
>   *(sage location!); what I wondered most*

like an Android or iPad on a nightstand
>   *was whether the sweetgum burrs and dried leaves*

grown footed for the purpose of bearing away
>   *were ornaments or accidents she interweaves*

any such device or gadget as may
>   *in the clearly golden silk, whose sub-webs*

distract him from a more pressing matter.
>   *are occupied by diminutive male sub-celebs*

Herse is perched on the precipice of the mattress
>   *holding down the fort (as she holds court)*

with its luxurious bedspread, where tapestry
>   *long after she vanishes, stopping short*

vis-à-vis itself interleaves the allegory.
>   *of the epiphany or apotheosis*

Real gold thread weighs the covers

     we expect from genteel arts, or a goddess

a cherub heaves to turn down for the lovers.

     "Who thereupon did rende the cloth in pieces every whit,

Would that the same in his wings might tip the scales,

     Bicause the lewdnesse of the Gods was biased so in it.

and with tears, put salt in these mythical tales

     And with an Arras weavers combe of Box she fiercely smit

by sinking level with us *l'enfant* in the room . . .

     Arachne on the forehead full a dozen times and more."

TROBAIRITZ (*ESTAT AI EN GREU COSSIRIER . . .*)

As the undisputed delivery system
for this pathogen,
you ought to be attending me,
not some wedding, indiscreetly
escorting a woman
past the nectariferous stamens

of a hundred lilies in their prime,
and your coupledom's.
Ill though I may be (with bronchitis
or love, probably both), I fight this
with the double rhythms
of weeding and wedding rhyme.

In the courtyard, unwanted outgrowths
are properly yanked.
I don't know what is less reminiscent of
the back-transformation of laurel into love
than outranked,
antiquated, turgid, infirm oaths!

The climbing rose ('Don Juan')
picks up where
the citrus leaves off—wintry lemon
giving way to a diabolic crimson
dunned from the air
of June, and making all months June.

Primavera's diktat: *Fiammante*. We have,
we are. I've tried
to avoid inflammation by poison ivy,
its dissembling look, its leaflets of three.
But as I pluck—triad
missing a harmonic stave—

I sing contagiously, so as not to cough.
So thirteenth-century of us:
we erase the *t*, the *i*, the *m*, the *e*
to quantify eternity
on a Catullian abacus.
It rains to occult the roving sun when we love.

TROUVILLE

Pissarro, who said we should raze the Louvre,
holds up; Renoir, not so much; Monet, yes:
especially *The Cliffs at Étretat*, viewed at some remove.
Tawny furze on Porte d'Aval, acuteness
of Needle Rock—those I can verify from memory.
The pinks Monet lavished on them disappear
if you stand across the room, where the lee
of evening is demarcated, clear.
It's one of the rules for viewing:
remembering that all those brushstrokes accruing
resolve at some distance, and become less rosy.

On a nearby wall, a tulip field reproduces that
tulip field we bicycled past in Texel,
and Étretat jogs the memory of the real Étretat.
So when we stop at your Corot, I wrestle
with the fables he makes of Fontainebleau.
What can Orpheus and Eurydice mean to us?
Can a painter make a non-space, and if so,
what relation to life does it have? Luteous
atmosphere of nymphs, representing a fiction
that is neither physics nor physician.
Would I rather another glimpse of what I know?

If you look very closely at that distant Trouville
beyond the boats coming into port, could you catch
a glimpse of us a dozen years ago, when our will
to true ourselves prevailed against mismatch?
See Orpheus and Eurydice with their averted faces.
If a painting meets our gazes, we are doomed.
But maybe ships' sails, depicted in real places,
are descendants of robed angels at Christ's tomb.
These Plexiglas skylights, modern as sans serif,
once provided access to the seraph.
And love as-is absorbed a gone oasis.

THREE DONNÉES

For he has forgotten self, forgotten bird . . .
SEAMUS HEANEY

A bittern! Belying this china-shop bird
    is, allegedly, a bull's
voice. Today it stalked the marsh for edibles,
    not a mate, so went unheard,

nearly unseen. What else did we reverse-hunt;
    let find us with sibylline
barbules prickling as it opened from its spine
    like a book?—then to confront

a waterlogged anhinga, hung out
    to dry in a branch of heaven
in the pose of Heaney's St. Kevin!
    Descending the birder's redoubt,

having glimpsed a heron's nest
    through another man's binoculars
and seen in the marsh's colors
    Netherlandish oils pressed

with gleams and inflections here and there,
    how could I resist when you said,
This green calls out for some red,
    to point out the cardinal pair

that came by way of reply—
    bearing in mind the sighs
at first sightings that vocalize,
    self-forgotten, a man's love cry?

The V's aggregate. I saw it:
    each configuration of cranes
        meeting another, aught
            elbows in pavanes
            that never linked;
        slippage as they kerned
    like printer's fonts, or pinked
what the prior flock patterned.

The unearthly guttural flutters
    you described were, at low altitude,
        flurrying in my ears—futures
            being told, shrewd
            proverbs translated
        from sandhills where migrations
    first originated:
Minutes from hours. Attrition of ions.

Was that mare made of plum blossom?
And her partner, the chestnut? Dark horse,
yes: he lingered in the shade as winsome
she ventured closer toward us.

A unicorn? "But unicorns don't exist,"
the younger brother told the older, an utter
role reversal. We edged as close to a tryst
as the fence would allow, were sugar

to melt in her mouth as it dusted her coat.
You and I, side by side, gaped at the vision
that materialized only after I thought
to ask for it, so it would seem given.

EPIC

It's you I'd like to see Greece again with;
you I'd like to take to a bed of cyclamen.
You know I nurse a certain myth
about myself—that I descend
de tribus d'origine asiatique
and am part Thracian or Macedonian,
cleaving to a Hellenic mystique
after centuries of migration inland.

FULL MOON over the Acropolis.
I can repeat the scene, this time à deux,
as then I had no one to kiss,
slicing halloumi amid the hullaballoo
of a rooftop taverna in July.
The doors that opened to lovers,
pulled like tree roots from darkness, I
close upon us now like book covers.

The alcove in which we embrace
is cool with brilliant tile
and weirded by a dove's note; chase

of ouzo with Uzi, junta-style.
History makes its noise; we duck
till it passes. Love we think is our due.
Not, we think, like the epoch,
the unchosen thing we're wedded to.

[MERRILL]

Who are you awaiting there, Psyche?

Night after night you dream you're lost
in some Alhambra, synecdoche
for all that's red and double-crossed
with ancient footfalls and heartache.

MIDNIGHT   The brownstone's sealed-off fireplace
contains a vase with a dried arrangement.
Corinthian columns (themes here are mixed)
rise to a motif of grape leaf and acanthus.
To the wall above it the landlord affixed
a baroque mirror, on the one hand meant
(in décor terms) to enlarge the narrow space,
and on the other to suggest a portal
to a world opposite and perhaps immortal,
which might (since it's *vacation*) open to us.

And, Psyche, isn't it piquant
that renovation started next door
just as you turned temporary resident?
The hammers and drills bore
(surprise surprise) just behind the mirror.

AUBADE   You, my luculent one . . .
    The sky, just restored to blue,
has in it a ghostly stone, blunted
    to a pearl-like lumen I have hunted,
if not to possess, then construe
    as my call to brighten . . .

When Eros abandons Psyche,
she wanders through Arcadia:
the hexagonal paths of the Park,
the opium purple façades of the Slope.
Pillowy undulations, earachy
echo chamber of bandstand and stadia,
craquelure of dry fountains, stark
contrast to "wellsprings of hope."

Combinatorics of sidewalk and subway:
Tilework. Hexagons (one station
even has neon ceiling hexagons
as part of an art installation).
And branching off in echelons
from orthotropic B'way,
miniature casbahs give every indication

of having wandered into an instance
of forbidden geometry (such as
begins with a fortress—not fort—
the feminine form!) in advance

of pool, gardens, palace.
Architecture for intrigues of court.
Hidden stairways. Whispering galleries
built on secret knowledge of ellipses . . .

(*Fort Da*, Psyche jokes to herself.)
. . . until what seem like fripperies
start to take on aspects of a universal
grammar. Repeated patterns tease
from arabesque and pentacle
and hexagon of course (the aleph
of this hivemind) 3-D airBn*Bs*.

"Nights are short but evenings come twice,
first under cover of a monsoon, causing
the untimely shine of a neighbor's porch light.
In order to stay with myself, on the advice
of thunder, like the bathers pausing,
ballplayers in the fields taking flight,

I turn the handle that resembles a key
and watch the filaments of a hurricane lamp
glow like an arachnid spliced with an isotope.
But the milk-glass lamp, so nineteenth-century
—an appliance for a barracks or a camp
retrofitted with a bulb, needs another trope.

It's not a sci-fi but a supernatural spider
englobed by two layers of the thinnest glass.
The supernatural is *literal*, derives
from *litter*. The dark knight. The ghost rider.
The portrait that speaks of what comes to pass.
Not a half-life: bric-a-brac of afterlives.

The box of books that shows up at my door
also has a supernatural quality to it.
I mailed it myself days ago, in another city.
I see my name as both addresser
and addressee—a type of blackmail. I let it sit
with all an unopened box's capacity.

On the train, zesting my ears, was a woman
whose speech seemed to flick from a syrinx.
Greenish the light from our filament-arachnid . . .
Taking my small refuse, a rusted garbage can
could tell I lived alone. Gleams on the links
of its chain leaped at me; I patted the lid."

SUNUP What to tackle first . . . There is
the vase of birthday flowers for instance.
Lily, aster, gerbera daisy, iris
need the ends of stems clipped, angled;
water refreshed; as though a second chance
at beauty could be wangled
out of a bit of maintenance.
Yet these dead birthday bouquets will be newfangled
again at your funeral, they promise.

It takes up quite a lot of acreage, all that sateen,
you thought, staring at an oil painting once.
When the dresses, jewels, lacework mean
to appear more painstaking than faces,
it's not for nothing that you make the inference.
At the table where the cut lemon graces
empty oyster shells, another may condense
on glass and pewter surfaces.
—*A woman's been painted out of this scene!*

Tiny the al fresco stage where one Ophelia (able)
and a Hamlet (decent) decant
their lines, as though a crucible
might be used as a cruet.
Medevac copters on their descent
periodically drown out Shakespeare's duet
near the hospital helipads, bent
on delivering meats (kidney, liver, heart)
cold, to furnish a second table.

EVENING   Measure out mixed grains
(quinoa, millet, bulgur, oat)
when a cardinal comes, disdains
to measure out his double note

but seems to understand his role
sorting lentils and seeds from ash,
as in fairy tales, to earn parole
and entrée to the prince's bash

for the incarcerated sister. He
peers through glass as quick
as eyes' saccades, or nicety
of the clock hand's uptick.

O sweet saccade. Cardinal—
we're past all parties. You have sorted
out of elementary particle
Song. All that's left to be courted.

"I forgot the gardens are free from ten to twelve.
Now it's almost one. The roses made people
happy. I saw them bending from the overlook,
small as bees but to less purpose. Each took
a page from a rhodocodex they can't reshelve.
Once opened, spines crack and sheaves spill.

Nothing is an accident in love or literature.
I came to the library for *The Aspern Papers*.
Not on the shelf. Not to be deterred,
I read 'Waiting for the Barbarians.' It appears
in retrospect that this was actually the apter
choice. (Thanks to the angel who commandeers
the signs that point to what to read. A lector
of one's own life is often what's required,
and I was lost in a confounding chapter.)

Even now it's dying, this season within a season,
neither spring nor summer. The temperatures
are climbing.   SOLSTICE   The heat will blossom
and the atmosphere sop up that solemn
almost-silence inside the cicadas' diapason,
abrading, day and night, stems and ligatures."

"Psyche, we your sisters see tons of noir
at Film Forum, and the repertoire
of betrayals includes this inadvertent one:
in *Under the Volcano*, the Consul is undone
when the Fascists find he's lied about his name
from Yvonne's love letters, which to his shame
he's never read. Like the rattlesnake embryo,
they send him to the bottom of the bottle-slash-arroyo."

Psyche had figured something less dire:

Doesn't it seem, my love, a bit supernumerary,
among the giddy tourists taking photos,
to have names staked beside the roses
of the Generalife? As if on tippy toes,
'Anna Pavlova' does the Sugar Plum Fairy.

(She'd tried to undermine his difficult *¿Quién sabe?*
with grammatical magic formulae. He would not give.

"Two ambiguities ought to make an affirmative,"
she quoted from the book. He hid a smile. *Maybe, baby.*)

"Dear Tenant,

Right before my husband left, he did me a good deed.
He hung a heavy mirror I had bought at an estate sale,
beveled, gilt, uncommonly clear. It was as though I'd freed
him to do what he neglects to do when chores entail
. . . what? Fairness? This was a gift. It hangs above eye level,
more to catch the light of the ceiling lamp than to reflect
the faces of his family back to them without him. The
    bubble
that equalizes, underwater, is a related concept:
It floats above us, waits to pop and flood us with relief.
An eye refusing to meet mine . . . When visiting the
    Freedom Tower,
window glass bristling from the bottom floors, wasn't a
    brief
glimpse of yourself promised amid the crowd, while the
    power
to withhold your reflection resided completely with . . ."

Here the letter breaks off; Psyche sees it begs

for closure of some sort, and adds: "No matter what, we
plummet.

The Tower, however, is insured, the way dancers insure
their legs.

I paid homage to the notion of Freedom by walking away
from it."

BLUE MOON   Dinner is dolmades from
the mini-mart. It seems the building sighed
out the men pounding on the mirror's other side.
They stand dazed, and look away—as if to come
at this hour with takeout signifies
a girl with a meaningless profession,
which doesn't pay to the extent it gentrifies.
She glances at the scaffold like a trellis
and hears a call to prayer in wrought iron:
"This is the real estate of the zealous."

El Cielo   The stained-glass skylight glows.
A letter awaits Psyche. *Dearest, j'arrive!*
And for a moment history is a vine
like a motif of grape that comes alive—

a thrill of drills and hammers coming close.

SU UNA LETTERA NON SCRITTA

I don't remember Crown Heights, arborists
to thin the rank on rank of leafy branch
that militated against the lighted street,
arresting a shadow with a history of priors,
that bouquets at the height of singing wires
might throw down gigantically at their feet.
I don't remember slicing my little tranche
of Brooklyn to hedge against my wrists.

. . . The ghost flush, or some such,
loose doorknobs, two keys: an empty station
of the cross where one lingers in extremity
waiting for emails. The designation *St.*
seemed like a reference to beatification
of neighborhoods where we'd never touch.

A LAST CONFESSION

The high priest dogwood swung his censer:
fragrant droplets bloomed mid-shower.
At the building's edge, the blue sky, denser
where you turn, behold the flower,

seems to indicate a threshold. Past that,
life could square with anything:
tortured petals, notched with flat
red daubs, improve the look of spring.

Thoughts of last night's movie follow suit—
the ballerina shot in pinks and grays.
Her dance along one tapering shoot;
her stigmata, leaping from pliés,

red, staining: toenail, fingernail—
where skin meets bark. She flayed
limbs, bent knee, beyond the pale,
chaste pith of laurel, née Daphne.

Our female Christ bent upon the bough
for bows? Applause, not Laws?
(I heard a female attorney avow
that ballet's anti-feminist. Strike for cause:

I'm offshoot of some like religious order.)
The dogwood darkens with sweat.
There's no turning back on the ordure
we rose from. Just a pirouette.

EPIPHANY LETTER

Because the sun set early, and I had no idea
where I was going, the night dropped, dear A.E.,
a plank of reflective dashes—Hansel's, pebble for pebble!—
and the stink of brine like diesel
rose up from either side, giving me to understand
I was driving over water. Or at least swampland.
When the moon turned up suddenly, a bead
on the Ravenel Bridge (for which misread:
composer of *Jeux d'eau*!), I thought it was training
its shadow on Boxing Day.
                    All this to say:
the mystery was borne, and I arrived, waning.

Perhaps I was a spy from Laurel Island . . .
I had passed it on my way, and wondered
if there was Isle of Oak as well as Bays
to round out the order of ancient honors.
As it was, I was traveling to the one for Palm.
(Military exploits.) Far now from the land
of Dollar This, Save That, Thrift Buys,
I found the house after some reconnoiters,

an exterior spiral staircase wafting like balsam
to a wheelhouse, and just under,
a window around an entire Christmas tree.
There you welcomed, introduced, and fed me.

Like the ocarinas your aunt baked from clay,
small holes under our bare feet may
have piped a tune by our quick passes.
A nighttime stroll, with wine and unbreakable glasses,
on the sand where everything is broken
by the tides—though the moon paring down, token
of our few days together, could also be a parable
of what fails to be irreparable.
Seems like nothing's gentle here but mist:
not spiky palms, sand spurs, the strigil
of a shell that scrapes the rock to grist;
not the lighthouse's gimlet vigil.

As in a fairy tale, there's a local Creole
so embargoed you've only heard it once,
and ever since (perhaps) the glimpse you stole
has worked a magic on you. You wince
when your daughter says *I winned*
but that her native tongue is not your own
is not as strange as that we mince
these words we're given. Rather say she's *wind*
—we can barely keep up! Or come down,
I think, from the enchantment of the epigone
toward this oceanic babble drawn and twinned.

Today you must have watched as the crucifix
was thrown, and the young men swam for it.
The consecration of the waters is on behalf
of a gentler god than the one
celebrated in the spumy upholstery
burst from you-know-who's seaborne throne.
As for us, I guess we like our stanzas

like barrier islands taking the hit

                    when the Atlantic's
all worked up in one of its blustery

                       dances,
and if it means to say *I winned*, we laugh.

WHAT TO READ THIS SUMMER

Terrible are the rose names . . .
Stakeholders in a tradition of
'Grande Amore' and 'True Love'
(one carmine, the other blush . . .), their aims

are, for the most part, scattershot.
'Mother's Day' and 'Playboy,'
'Senior Prom' and 'Let's Enjoy'
vie with a lyrical 'Lady of Shalott,'

while a flyweight 'Pink Knockout'
comes 'Outta the Blue' to mock
'Honey Perfume,' 'Pillow Talk'
—jock Cupid wielding clout.

Then maybe a puckish curator
pairs 'Las Vegas' with 'Nearly Wild,'
'Buttercream' with 'Julia Child,'
'Aloha' with 'Hello, Neighbor . . .'

★

Misenus, son of Aeolus, god of the wind,
don't you think it's bad form
to practice trumpet on this platform,

what with the dentistry squeal
at construction-site decibel levels
of braking blade shaving molar steel,

dropped-in blare of delays and arrivals
squelched against granite, at close intervals,
while you riff on "Over the Rainbow"?

You received some negative attention
from Triton, after blowing his conch so loud
you inadvertently entered yourself

in an unwinnable contest; now,
stuck in a twenty-first-century translation
of hell, you press the stops, and for an obol

prepare our burial in an infinite axial scroll
with a tinier and tinier turning radius,
as if we were those hordes, the unsanctified,

who shoved one another along the Cocytus,
none led on to the golden bough
by Venus's semaphore, the unloved rock doves,

whom Virgil treats so gently in the *Aeneid*.

CYTHERA

Here where the girls wear a tattoo flower
with pink hair, their lower halves
dissolving not into the old fishtails
of mermaid lore, but whatever horsepower
unites their noir leather-clad calves
with a noir chassis, over softails,

I see centauresses alongside last century's
signage (think "The Mediterranean,"
or Resort, Lodge, Manor, Condo,
presaged with "Ocean Breeze").
Customized with LED neon,
their insides outside, like the Pompidou,

they've stolen the show. The seashore
at evening, swept flat as an ice rink;
the gull, folding its wings like the tabs
of take-out cartons (the waves as usual bore
out predictions, cracking, with a wink,
shellfish—like fortune cookie grabs);

the frigate birds, light as zinc,
strong-armed by the "ocean breeze"
(walking in the turgid surf is difficult
and, you'd think,
might disabuse us of the pleasantries
attributed to Aphrodite's cult);

all the original instinct for display or chase
from which this performance rises
(or depends) carries on life-and-death
while our species looks at its own face,
experimenting with disguises,
putting time on hold by holding its breath.

A HORSE DOES NOT

WANT TO BE FEDEXED

Beauty is a fight to the finish,
though you want to educate
the decorum away. Here,
in the bruised atmosphere
of a tropical storm, we wait
for the rainband to diminish,

considering horses. Your student
had one shipped from Holland.
"A horse does not want to be FedExed."
(Could one apply dressage to text?
Have it perform at one's command?
Banish felicitous accident?)

★

"You have to be a perfectionist,"
she had noted. Discipline
is stylish, but there's a grace

by which your hands displace
the eye of the storm within
the encirclement of my wrist,

and how say that, much less
transmit it? Along the coast,
the tempest is elegant, like something
bred for show jumping
across state lines, almost
—no, really—over distress.

★

The scent of a broken twig
increasing a hundredfold:
the perfume of a living limb
exhaling, at the jagged enjamb-
ment, its last. All told,
the damage caused is as big

as that of any grown tree
striking the edge of the roof,
bouncing on the fence—
tripping off calls to insurance,
prayers to limbs still aloof,
and recognition of mercy.

★

A fight to the finish, "sunlight
on the garden," rain-lacquered,
hurricane-groomed.
The roses gave a start and bloomed
like silly. If we've acquired
a taste for drama, an appetite

for tropical depression follows.
—And so we clown.
I saw the fresh wood up; it awes
me to see the parasites and moss
studding the victor's crown
that brought down the house.

NOTES ON THE POEMS

Most of these poems were written in and about Lebanon, Texas, and Florida. The myths of Orpheus and Eurydice, and Cupid and Psyche, subtend the book. "Epic" owes a particular debt to James Merrill's Psyche poem, "From the Cupola," as well as the mathematical concept of "forbidden symmetry." Byblos is the site of one of the oldest written inscriptions in a real alphabet (Phoenician). "Frontier" is indebted to *Aransas: The Life of a Texas Coastal County* by William Allen and Sue Hastings Taylor, as well as Frederick Law Olmsted's Texas journal. "Captivity" quotes from Mary Rowlandson's captivity narrative, and links it to the story of Rachel Plummer. "In the gods" is a term for theater seats in the upper balcony; the poem refers to the Houston Grand Opera's production of *Das Rheingold*, and "Marriage as Baroque Music" quotes from Ernst Christoph Homburg's poem as reproduced in Buxtehude's *Liebster, meine Seele saget* (performed by Ars Lyrica Houston). "Revelations" makes use of Goethe's *Italian Journey.* "They That Dally with Words May Soon Make Them Wanton" touches on Shakespeare's *Twelfth Night*, as "Knot Garden" does *Much Ado About Nothing.* "Hershey Suite" borrows a line from Milton's "On the Late Massacre in Piedmont," with reference to Pennsylvania's history of religious freedom. "Two Hangings from Ovid" quotes Arthur Golding's translation of Ovid, and describes a tapestry in the Metropolitan Museum of Art, "Aglauros's Vision of the Bridal Chamber of Herse, from the Story of Mercury and Herse." "Trouville" describes Monet's *Cliffs at Étretat* in the same museum, and Corot's *Orpheus and Eurydice* at the Frick. "Trobairitz" winks at the twelfth-century woman troubadour the Comtessa de Dia. "Su una Lettera Non Scritta" steals a line from Eugenio Montale. "What to Read This Summer" contains a nod to Seamus Heaney's translation of Book VI of the *Aeneid*. "Epiphany Letter" is dedicated to A. E. Stallings, with thanks to Dr. Frances Anderson for her hospitality. Decision theory, according to the *Stanford Encyclopedia of Philosophy*, "is concerned with the reasoning underlying an agent's choices, whether this is a mundane choice between taking the bus or getting a taxi, or a more far-reaching choice about whether to pursue a demanding political career." "Distant mandate" is a phrase from László Krasznahorkai's *Seiobo There Below,* speculating on the obscure origins of the Alhambra and, by extension, art itself.

ACKNOWLEDGMENTS

I owe a debt of gratitude to the editors who published these poems in the following journals:

The American Scholar: "Three Données"

Granta: "Revelations"

Literary Imagination: "Marriage as Baroque Music"

Little Star: "In the Gods," "Milkweed," "Listening Posts," "Hershey Suite," "Trouville," "A Last Confession"

London Review of Books: "Gelsenkirchen," "Dear Tenant, . . . ," "BLUE MOON . . ."

The Nation: "Captivity"

The Paris Review: "Breeze Blocks in the Wild Hollyhocks," "Trobairitz"

Parnassus: "Knot Garden," "Epiphany Letter," "Cythera"

Poetry: "Cottonmouth," "Frontier," "The Fort," "They That Dally Nicely with Words May Quickly Make Them Wanton," "It's you I'd like to see Greece

again with . . . ," "Borrowed Bio," "Two Hangings
from Ovid," "What to Read This Summer"

The Southern Review: "Cooked in Their Own Ink,"
"Nights are short but evenings come twice, . . ."

In particular, the support of the following editors over the
years has been a great encouragement to me: John Palattella,
Christian Wiman, Don Share, Robyn Creswell, Ann Kjellberg,
Daniel Soar, Jessica Faust, Herb Leibowitz. Thanks to my kind
and canny colleagues at the University of Houston and the
University of Florida. Thanks to Jonathan Galassi and Carolina
Baizan for reading every word, and interrogating every comma.

I also wish to thank Edward Hirsch and the Guggenheim
Foundation for a fellowship that funded the time needed to
write and revise many of the poems in this book. I am very
grateful for it.

Much love to my sons for their gentleness and gusto.

Love to Michael, Alicia.